Animal World

THE HARE

translated by
Erica and Arthur Propper

illustrated by
Patrick Oxenham

Macdonald Educational

Three baby hares

A female hare has built a comfortable nest for her young at the edge of the wood. She is called a 'doe'. Her nest is a 'form'. She has made it out of dry grass, using her hind-legs to shape it. She has lined it with down that she has pulled off her belly.

Here you see the hare's three babies. They were born not long ago, but their eyes are already open and their long ears twitch. They have golden-brown fur and it is difficult to see them in the grass. Their black noses are moist and quivering. They are very timid young animals.

At night

During the day the hare goes off to feed, or browse, in the field. At night she returns to feed her young. They take enough milk to last them until the next night.

They are already able to walk and run, and can even make their own 'forms' near to their mother's. But she will not let them stir from their 'forms' during the day. If they did they could easily be killed by foxes or weasels, for they cannot defend themselves.

The first outing

The young hares are now twelve days old.
They are ready to run and jump about, and
to taste the plants that their mother feeds
on.

　　They learn from her which plants are
the most tender and have the best flavour.
One of the tastiest is a herb called thyme,
but fresh mint and marjoram are good too.
The young hares eat until they are
satisfied. Afterwards they leave small,
round droppings on the ground.

The alarm signal

While the young hares are busy cutting through the plants with their small, sharp teeth, the doe keeps a watchful eye on things around them. Her ears are cocked to catch the slightest sound of danger. Magpies, buzzards, crows and rooks are flying near. They are all birds that kill and eat young hares.

The doe has a special alarm signal to warn her babies of danger. She displays her white tail. At once, each young hare rolls itself into a ball and keeps close to the ground. With its golden colour, it is very hard to see against the soil and plants. The birds do not dare attack the doe, and fly away.

9

In the dark

Although they are so timid, the young hares are not afraid of dark nights. They prefer to go out at night and sleep during the day.

They are all on their own now. The doe has left them, for she no longer needs to help them feed and hide. She has taught them about the food that they can find in the kitchen garden. They go out every night in search of vegetables to eat. They especially like turnips, carrots, parsley and radishes. Here, they are nibbling at some tasty, fresh turnips.

An attack

One night when it is very hot, the young hares scamper
into the kitchen garden through a hole that their mother
has dug under the fence. They settle down to eat the
vegetables and their stomachs get bigger and rounder.
Suddenly, they hear a strange noise. A cloud of droning
mosquitoes comes swooping down on them.

    The hares are afraid and they try to hop away, but the
mosquitoes follow them. They attack and sting the hares
on their noses and inside their ears. The poor little hares
take shelter in some bushes. They feel better after they
have licked their stinging noses and rested in the cool
grass, well away from the mosquitoes.

Another danger

In autumn the hares have another danger to face. This is the season for hunters to go out with their guns and their dogs.

The young hares have only two ways of defending themselves— by keeping very still in their 'forms' or by running away very fast. They can run at speeds of up to 70 kilometres an hour. They make huge leaps and swerves to throw the dogs off the scent.

Into the water

One of the young hares suddenly feels the ground falling away beneath his feet. Something cold and wet closes over his body. He has fallen into a pond.

His legs start to move at once and he paddles strongly. He knows how to swim without being taught. Once he is in the water the dogs cannot pick up his scent. The hare swims safely across the pond, back to the others.

13

Autumn

Happily, the hunting season will soon be over and the hunters will go home. Their dogs will go with them and the hares will feel safe again. The dogs terrify them because they can keep up the chase with their keen sense of smell.

Hares change colour slightly in the autumn. Their fur becomes more grey to match the furrows in the fields where they hide. They also have bigger appetites. They need to eat more and put on enough fat to last them through the winter.

Snow

When the snow comes the hare has to be very careful. His tracks show up in the soft snow and other hungry animals may try to hunt him down.

He digs a hole under the snow and crouches in it. He does not move. His thick fur swells to keep him warm. He takes short, quick breaths. The warm air he breathes out melts the snow, and a little hole is left in it. This is the one sign that a hare is hiding.

Everything is covered with snow. Life is now difficult for the hare. When the snow has stopped falling he must take the risk of leaving his hiding-place. He is too hungry not to. Covering the ground in little leaps, he sets out for the kitchen garden. He looks under the snow for any vegetables that might have been left behind.

A find

The hare can tell by his sense of smell that there are still some turnips in the ground under the snow. He digs them up with his paws.

But unlike some other animals, he is not able to carry food home with him. Because of this, he has to make his dangerous journey across the snow several times. If he didn't he would have no food at all and then he would die of hunger.

Spring

Winter is over at last. Spring has come and at night a full moon lights up the fresh grass.

The hares have come out of their hiding-places. Now they are dancing through the fields. They are happy and excited. They squeak loudly. As they nibble at the tender young shoots, their energy returns.

They get rid of their dirty winter coats by rubbing themselves against the trees. Underneath, their fur is new and shiny.

They play for hours, chasing each other and leaping in the air. With all this exercise their weakened muscles become strong again.

Boxing

It is in spring that the young males begin to box with each other. They stand up on their hind-legs and punch with their paws. They also bite.

This happens in March. It is the only time in the year that they behave in this way. They suddenly change from being the timid creatures that they usually are. With the coming of spring, they have new energy.

The young hares now weigh two kilograms and will grow even bigger and heavier.

A mating

The male hare meets a doe. They sniff each other very timidly at first. Then they rub muzzles, and when they have become friends, they mate.

As time goes on the doe grows stouter. She is going to have babies. She will have three more litters during the summer. But by then the hare will have left her. He is not interested in his offspring. He leaves them in the care of their mother.

It is summer now and the hares have finished their games. They have become timid again and are always ready to hide or run away. At night they will go wandering and during the day they will take shelter.

Some interesting facts

There are 24 species of hares. This book describes the brown, or European, hare. From birth the young hares which are called leverets, can see well, but only for short distances.

The hare lives for eight to twelve years. Behind its main teeth it has two small cutting teeth, called incisors, in the upper jaw.

It has very long hind-legs. When it runs the powerful muscles of the legs throw it forward. The forelegs touch the ground together and it takes off again. This is a kind of bounding gallop.

When it is attacked it defends itself by changing direction as it runs away. The soles of its feet are covered with a thick layer of hair which wears out in old age.

The fully grown hare is 70 centimetres long and weighs four kilograms. The hairs of its fur are joined together by small links. These make the fur waterproof.